A Hudson Landscape

PHOTOGRAPHS BY WILLIAM CLIFT

A Hudson Landscape

PHOTOGRAPHS BY WILLIAM CLIFT

Prose Companion by Paul Kane

WILLIAM CLIFT EDITIONS · SANTA FE, NEW MEXICO

STORM KING MOUNTAIN FROM COLD SPRING

Prose Companion

by Paul Kane

The Hudson is a drowned river, whelmed by the tidal reaches of the Atlantic. Once, anciently, it flowed out beyond the continental shelf, nearly halfway to Bermuda—its vestige known now as the Hudson Canyon. With its precipitous shores, the river might well be called the Hudson Fjord, were it not for the continuous tribute of headwaters, reaching far back to Lake Tear of the Clouds on Mt. Marcy in the Adirondacks.

~~~~~~~~~

The Hudson is a river of large gestures and subtle effects. It moves in a landscape of its own creation, and creates in its movement a mode of existence, a distinct locality and habitation. It is a river to grow up with, for it marks, in all its variable features, the type of all rivers: long and deep in its course; dominant in its enfolding landscape; and, at its terminus, serene in the broad sweep of ocean bays. For those who live near it, the Hudson is a familiar spirit, welcoming in its steady, even sturdy, beauty, while at the same time unsettling in the way it holds one at a distance, the shores complex and often inaccessible. Few rivers make such warrantable impressions. Through the Highlands, in particular—where it runs the deepest—depths are answered by the steep western heights of Bear Mountain, Crows Nest, and Storm King. On the opposite shore, near Garrison and Cold Spring, the hills step back in more modest undulations, leaving marshes, ponds and islands on the margins, before the ascent to the high scarpes of Bull Hill and Breakneck Ridge. There is, about the river, an equipoise—it seems to balance the landscape and embellish it, the way clouds can sometimes lend character and depth to the sky.

The Highlands, traditionally, has been an area invested with words —images and legends elicited by the landscape have made it a locale where myth and history coincide with our sense of the dramatic: the Heer, or Imp, of the Dunderberg; Captain Kidd's treasure; the *chevaux-de-frise*, or iron chains, at West Point; the treason of Benedict Arnold. As with the very deepest point in the river—the place known as "World's End"—what we cannot fathom we mythologize. Anyone who stops to consider the river is likely to make a myth of time out of its constant flow of water.

It is along these highland shores, too, that the river seems in conversation with itself and its surroundings. The way the Hudson twists and in its turnings establishes discrete sections—as if the river were a series of separate lakes, some narrow between cliffs, others a mile wide and open to the sky—is like a succession of moods and musings, reflections on the fortunes of time, all in the light of a human activity that traffics in roads and railroads, that throws elegant bridges across the water.

The Hudson is graced with magnificent bridges. The George Washington Bridge, Bear Mountain Bridge, the Mid-Hudson, the Rip Van Winkle—these are bridges of active imaginings. There is purposeful grandeur to them, and—with the exception of the one at Tappan Zee, with its long bending sweep—they are all suspended from stunning heights. One thinks of them as wrought in an age of steel, when New York was industry itself and manufactured wealth, legendary wealth. Bridges like the Bear Mountain are meant as vivid acts, executed in sublime surroundings in response to an inner need to endow our outer deeds with a sense of the lofty, the exhilarating. Seen from a distance, especially from a point above, they seem to exemplify our most lyrical moments. To suspend a road from twin towers, with knitted cables of fine steel, is an inspired, even precarious idea. You need only walk across one of these bridges on a windy day, high above the whitecaps below, to feel in the sway and bounce of the bridge the precise calculations of engineered feats of beauty.

But for all the drama of the Hudson and its environs, there is an understated quality throughout that gives it, for many, the feel of time. The mountains here are nearly a billion years old, and their rounded summits are witness to their age. Among them, you think: only something so old could be so calm.

~~~~~~~~

Just south of Bear Mountain Bridge, in mid-river, lies Iona Island. Walking around it is like deciphering a palimpsest: its separate histories superimposed like layers of imperfectly erased writing. Once a major vineyard and orchard, then a summer resort, later a U.S. Naval Arsenal, it is now a wildlife sanctuary. An overgrown road, the remains of a concrete foundation, a dismantled fence: again, we see how time and nature rescind our acts.

On Iona, at high tide, the river smells of the sea. Gulls follow the water course as if the Hudson were a natural map. Only here, forty miles upstream, do the sea breezes that ease Iona's climate die out. Spring comes to the island weeks earlier than upstream at Newburgh. Dolphins used to visit these waters regularly, which must have given the place an even milder aspect. On the high knolls of Iona, among lichened granite outcrops, you can find prickly pear cacti luxuriating in the sun. There are deer on the island; they may have swum over from either shore. Even squirrels will swim the Hudson. Canada geese inhabit the coves, some perched on submerged rocks; chipmunks abound, visible only in their scamper; songbirds, in the meadows, seem unconcerned. Walking the woods alone here, it is easy to feel clumsy and noisy, as if a profane intruder on sacrosanct land. But

spook a family of deer nearby and their crash and flight will startle the whole island.

Between the shore and the island extends the Iona Bird Sanctuary, a marshland divided by the Snake Hole Creek into Salisbury Meadow and Ring Meadow. The Doodletown Brook—met by the Timp Brook—comes down off the high hills into the marsh and gives its name to the Doodletown Bight, a small cove formed by the northwest spur of the island. Wild rose-mallow, with showy pink and red blossoms, stand along the fringes among cattails and arrow arum and pickerel-weed. Looked at from above, the tall grasses make herringbone textures and complex striated patterns. When the breezes are light, the wind moves through the meadow so gently it all seems to breathe, and the round flat hummocks become momentary swells and dilations. In its fullness, the whole of the meadow is rich, dank, and fertile, alive with every shade and degree of summer green that shimmers.

Iona Island is located in "The Race," a section of the Hudson that runs from a point above Peekskill to Bear Mountain. As with most places along the Hudson, it has had several names in the past, and one, "Devil's Horse Race," underscores the sailor's view of the river here: the channel between Manitou and Dunderberg, and Anthony's Nose and Bear Mountain, narrow and deep; the trick winds off the mountains treacherous; the downstream current the swiftest anywhere on the river. Few sailboats venture these waters, though motorboats bob in repose. "A decent respect for the Hudson would confine us to use of the boat," says Henry James, and the summer tour boats, with their green canopies and festive flags, ply this reach of the river best seen from the river itself. Respect is also called for by the *genius loci*, the Dunderberg imp, whose domain extends upriver as far as Pollepel Island. Washington Irving records that "regular skippers of the river for a long time did not venture to pass the Donder Berg without lowering their peaks, out of homage to the Heer of the Mountains." With the Dunderberg (or "Thunder Mountain") to the south and Storm King to the north, the Highlands is bounded by cautions.

From the top of Bear Mountain, topography becomes natural history. The Hudson, dividing the Appalachian chain at sea level, carves its way through geological ages. In their expanse, the surrounding mountains restore a sense of horizon—and where lower down they hem you in with twisting roads through forests, here they release you to the sky. And where you were walking only a short while before, you look upon now as from a great distance, as would a stranger noting someone's movements dispassionately. You mark the hawks, below you, drifting up the declivities. And the constant surface patterns the river makes, with its currents and channel eddies, with the wakes of boats and the attentions of the wind, seem like a script you could almost read. You note the complexity of the shoreline; you see how the river insinuates the shore.

〰〰〰〰〰

In the geography of mind, mountains represent sublime moments. They stand out as features of our experience, endowed with the character of permanency. It is not just a matter of loftiness—the highest, or most intense, is often the least interesting, the most fleeting—rather, we are struck more by the deep impression of solidity, of force, and by the isolate shape of power. These experiences range across the landscape of our memory. There are mountains in nature that likewise convey a presence out of proportion to their size—they are like a force field attracting our attention: one thinks of Mt. Monadnock in New Hampshire; Diamond Head on Oahu; Shiprock in New Mexico; and along the Hudson, as the northwest buttress to the Highlands, Storm King.

Although not as high as either Crows Nest adjacent to the south or Breakneck Ridge across on the eastern shore, Storm King dominates this section of the river known as Martyr's Reach. Coming up the Hudson, the mountain appears to step out from the Highland chain to take precedency. The Clove, the deep valley separating Storm King from Crows Nest, allows for the full shape of the mountain to appear,

giving it a distinctness other peaks lack. Once past this point, the river again opens out to a wide expanse, as Storm King marks the northern terminus of the Highlands.

These mountains, geologically, are part of the Reading Prong, formed in the Precambrian era. Originally, they would have been of spectacular height, but cyclic erosion and the climatic Pleistocene ice sheet wore them down to their present granite and gneissic core. A scramble through the woods here reveals numerous rock knobs—what the French call *roches moutonnées* (or "fleece rocks")—bedrock outcrops, smoothed and polished over time, with one side gently sloping out of the ground and the other scarped abruptly. Climbing the back of Storm King, negotiating these rocks, you realize they are themselves versions of the mountain, replicas in miniature of the larger, corresponding outline of Storm King itself.

A narrow road, two hundred feet above the river, cuts along the face of the mountain. The road creates a lip, discernible from a distance. On the precipitous eastern front, you can pull off the road and view Cold Spring and Little Stony Point downriver, with Newburgh and the fabled Pollepel Island to the north. It was here that a public utility planned to build a hydroelectric plant which would have defaced Storm King and scarred the eastern hills (already damaged by quarrying in the nineteenth century). The project was stopped by public opposition. The one argument the utility could not answer was the aesthetic one, which carried its own imperative. What made Storm King so valuable was, in the words of Vincent Scully's testimony, "the fact that it preserves and embodies the most savage and untrammeled characteristics of the wild at the very threshold of New York. It can still make the city dweller emotionally aware of what he most needs to know: that nature still exists, with its own laws, rhythms, and powers, separate from human desires."

Upriver, around the bend from Storm King, is Cornwall-on-Hudson. Viewed from the landing, where local pleasure boats are harbored, the river once more takes on the appearance of an extensive lake, as it widens out into Newburgh Bay. From the impetus of wind and boat traffic, the waves breaking on the stony riverside have the wash and regularity of an ocean. After the sublimity of the close Highlands, the river here seems easy, open and hospitable. Families sit at picnic tables in the park; a sloop sail picks up the shape of the receding hills; even Storm King, from this side, appears less dominant. But as you move inland, the mountain begins to take on another aspect. The land evens out, rolling back into the Great Valley, and from the north and west side, Storm King, as the portal to the Highlands, becomes visible intermittently for miles. On the roads winding through the immediate countryside, the mountain comes into view suddenly and from various angles. And once again, the mountain begins to be felt as a presence: monumental, primitive, sovereign. Long afterwards, you carry its impression.

~~~~~~~~~

The Hudson drains the country it runs through, as if calling to itself the attendant streams, creeks and nearby ponds. It is an imperious river, stately in its slow movement, as in a procession or a progress. The homes, factories, landings that press the banks of the river are like moments in a timeline in motion. Defunct buildings line it, throwbacks to an earlier economy, and even the mansions of the gilded rich —Vanderbilts, Rockefellers, Roosevelts (for whom to sight the river was to appropriate it)—are now themselves commemorations of the way time disinherits us. The river seems to accept such homage. Unlike man, water is always in its element.

Thales, the ancient Greek philosopher, thought everything reducible to the one element, water. The world began in water, was sustained by water, and the earth itself floated in water. He was more right, perhaps, than he knew. We ourselves are mostly water, and what is water but process and change? Sunlight glistens on the river; mist rises like steam; clouds lower; ice floes pile up thick along the shore. Where water goes, so go we.

We are drawn to water by a more than ancient memory, for we all live by water. It comes to us in various and appropriate guises. A stream, a brook, a rivulet, or a rill is a child's companion throughout the year: water moving in narrow banks on a shallow bed, from somewhere obscure above to somewhere below. Rivers, large ponds, lakes and oceans are more presences than companions, more features of the outer world than reflections of desire. We grow into them. Large bodies of water ask deeper questions, and deflect easy answers. The fisherman, casting his line, is an emblem of us all. We catch ourselves thinking along new channels when we stand by the water's edge. We feel the old pull.

A water course carries the sky on its surface, and we delight in the intermixture of colors and shapes, and the play of light that marries our moods to the visual surroundings. To reflect, says the river, is to bend back. Water gives us the perfected image of our world—a world of the first water.

~~~~~~~~~

Along the west bank of the Hudson, above Newburgh Bay, hills rolling toward the river are planted with orchards and vineyards. The good drainage and good soil are favorable to the varieties of fruit trees and grape vines. In the fall, at roadside stands, you take your pick: Macintosh, Delicious, Cortland, Macoun, Jonagold, Northern Spy, Ida Red, Empire, Winesap, Mutsu—fifty kinds of apples in all. The growers are connoisseurs here and will discourse at length on the relative values of each apple, culminating always with a paeon to their favorite. One woman urges Macouns—with a taste like sharp wine— though they don't keep very long. In the blaze of October, this area is a paradise of color, with every tree declaring itself in the inverse of its leaving. Spring here is Edenic too, with white and pinkish-white blossoms carpeting the hills, like an immense formal garden in an innocent land.

Wineries flourish as well. A small bottle of local sweet wine with dessert can seem a distillation of all that is memorable in a season. And a few ripe grapes off the vine makes one think we could live on so little. The migrant workers, gathered on the landing of a warehouse early on a cold morning, know better.

This section of the mid-Hudson was once a center for raspberry growing. Every day a boatload of raspberries would depart from Marlboro for New York, filling the river for miles with an unmistakable aroma. Just north, in Milton, a Quaker colony prospered, growing grapes, raspberries, currants and strawberries. The inner light tradition must have found a salutary reflection in the suffusion of sunlight that so attracted the Hudson River School painters and the Luminists that followed. There are still some Quaker farms in the area.

An old family farm is like an obstruction in a stream, forming a pool of slowly swirling water around which the rest of the stream rushes. On a farm, the wheel of time spins on the axis of nature. To plant, to grow, to harvest, to repair in winter—and occasionally, to let lie fallow—takes long thoughts and recurring dreams. A *livelihood*, in its root sense, is a "leading" or a "way to life," and a *farm* derives from a word meaning "durable." Things last on a farm; you find a way to go on—a way of life. An old shed, dilapidated, is shored up enough to use another season. The tractor, jerryrigged, keeps going. What looks casual is more studied than you might suppose—and the long view is what resolves contradictions here.

There are people in small villages along the Hudson that seem part of the land's texture and its rhythm—as if the pace of the river sets the pace of their own lives. You can stop and talk awhile and not feel rushed or obtrusive. A man in his seventies picks, in a desultory way, through the burnt rubble of a once-magnificent barn. Vaulted rafters, a slate roof, a pair of cupolas—a family pride—now heaped, charred and twisted. For him every fragment, every object is a shard of memory; he wishes it had all been consumed rather than this piecemeal dying he must live by. An ox shoe his father had uncovered in a field; a wooden wheel to a young boy's makeshift wagon; antique tools; an

antique car: nothing is wholly destroyed, nothing wholly preserved. He just wishes it would all go away. Nearby, an old fruit tree, all but dead, seems a reproach. The man recites some lines from the Quaker poet, Whittier—the famous "saddest" words: "It might have been." He turns and walks home to his mid-day meal.

〰〰〰

From Hyde Park south to Stony Point, the central Hudson is paralleled on both sides by railroad tracks, with freight moving on the west bank and passenger trains on the eastern side. While standing on a hillside, it is not unusual to see one train heading north and on the opposite side another one going south. The passenger trains are short and sleek, flashing by with a silver intensity. They pique our curiosity. But there is something more compelling about a long slow freight train, its motley assemblage of cars hailing from as far away as Atlanta or Santa Fe—carrying who knows what?—and the whole variegated conveyance wending along the curving shoreline, seemingly taking its time to reach the destined freightyard. There is still a longing to be felt in a distant whistle, though it's heard now not as a beckoning call—as in one's youth—but as a sound the past makes in its passing. There are times when a train whistle can make life itself seem like a Doppler effect. Trains carry a freight of memories. The railroad was always an amiable way to travel. A young boy, in mid-summer—in mid-century—sits on the wicker seat of an open car, opposite his grandfather with his straw hat and seersucker suit: it is a trip from Poughkeepsie to New York and as exotic for him then as any traveling since. With the Hudson level and close on the right and trackbeds and embankments on the left—and beyond them houses and people (so many lives!)—the world moves by in parallel lines.

In a landscape, a river divides the world. Moving in that landscape, you are always located in reference to the river, either on one side or another, and this comes to affect how you think of the world and how you see it: everything appears to have its complement, its counterpart, as if the river were the inspiration for the way we plow furrows in a field, or plant an orchard or a garden, for the way a road is divided or tracks laid down, for the way one person seeks to answer another. Even objects take on a new sense in this parallel world. Bean poles, a rail fence, a wooden ladder, are all symmetries to the eye.

In its double suggestiveness of ascent and descent, a ladder is one of our most metaphorical tools. But a day on a ladder is not easily forgot. In "After Apple-Picking," Robert Frost remarks: "My instep arch not only keeps the ache,/ It keeps the pressure of a ladder-round." For all our mobility, we are as awkward climbing as we are crawling on our hands and knees. We do best upright on the horizontal. We prefer to have our two feet firmly planted on the ground, which may be why we so often compare ourselves with trees: rooted and growing, possessing a trunk and limbs, living in a forest of people, or related to others as part of a family tree. We like having trees around us—they lend a congruency to our lives. As with so many other things, a tree is a double of itself—its roots mirror its branches. A poet once said that "The trees encountered on a country stroll/ Reveal a lot about a country's soul." They can also say a lot about individuals. In a river valley like the Hudson, the person who cultivates an apricot or a cherry tree has a different sense of time than one who keeps a pair of yews.

~~~~~~~

As you move north from below the Mid-Hudson Bridge through the bend in the river known as Crum Elbow, and then further, past Esopus Island and Rhinecliff and Kingston, and up to the tidal flats of Saugerties—a stretch of the river known to the Dutch captains as Lange Rack or Long Reach—the Hudson seems more sedate and even, as the countryside around it flattens out in low plateaus that offer wide horizons and contemplative views up and down the river. This is the area of the Hudson associated with mansions and estates, with aristocratic manors and colonial patents. Here a certain serenity in the landscape appealed to those seeking their own versions of contentment or complacency, and the buildings and gardens encountered along the embankments have a formality that would be out of place in the more rugged and dramatic regions of the river. Homes here have names: Crum Elbow, Wildercliff, Wilderstein, Ellerslie, Rokeby, Wrongside, Clermont. At times, it seems that the river accommodates these structures—and the landscaped gardens that accompany them—as a grownup tolerates and humors the make-believe of children. The angular projections of the man-made diminish before the smooth immensity of water and rounded hills and overall sky. But nature has its own angularities: a tree juts out a limb sharply at a right angle, silhouetted against an afternoon whiteness; a granite cliff face drops in sheer degrees; a point of land dislocates a flow of river water. And yet by such juxtapositions—by differences—we come to know the continuities of the river, the sense of its unchanging flux.

A river, even one as memorable as the Hudson, is subject to the fluxions of our concern. When the shad run upstream in the spring, the river teems with elemental memory, but in the small towns and villages along its banks, there is always the danger of forgetting, of dismembering, the past. What is given us is what we take for granted; and what we take for granted is often taken away. That is the lesson of the river. We speak at times of a flood of memories, as if a river running through us had overflowed its banks. But the act of memory goes against the flow of time, and the further back we go—as if returning upstream to a source—the less we can recall, until there comes a time when there is nothing but a blank of years, a rapids we cannot negotiate and must abandon at last.

~~~~~~~

There is a Dutch legend connected with Blue Point, a jut of land "a little drink" up the river from Milton on the western shore. The ghostly "Storm Ship," which would appear suddenly on the river, sailing in moonlight and heedless of the weather, was said to have its anchorage at Blue Point, or as it was called then, Juffrouw's Hoeck. I think of it now as marking the spot across the river where my grandparents laid out the family plots in the Poughkeepsie Rural Cemetery. There, on summer evenings, fireflies out over the water phosphoresce.

The Hudson is an elegiac river, linked forever with our sense of the past. Every name of every point on the river is a story in itself, if we recuperate the past and make it part of our present knowing. But the river is also something we cannot name and can only know in the immediacy of its presence. And here, too, we make an icon of the river: light and water, shadow and mass, and the human desire to adhere to the world we live in, a world—a landscape—the Hudson shapes around us. We look to the elements of our world, the common and familiar objects we know so well, to denominate our lives. Our seeing, when we are truly seeing, is of our seeing. And we come to know the feel of a place by inhabiting our vision of it. We may look to others to tell us what they see, but in the end, we make a landscape of our own.

~~~~~~~~~~

The Hudson is a river of the moon and sun—of the solar and lunar oscillations of the ocean. "The-Water-That-Flows-Two-Ways" the Algonkins called it, seeing the inrushing tide reverse the downward flow. The tidal crest travels ten hours upstream, where the water rises two feet, and the salt point that shifts from season to season shifts with diurnal tides as well. Moving down with the current, moving up with the tide, a piece of wood will take a year to float to the sea. Once, primordial, the Hudson was two rivers, separated by the Appalachian divide, until the god Manitou—legend has it—became angry at profligate men and drowned them, cleaving the Highlands from Storm King down to Bear Mountain.

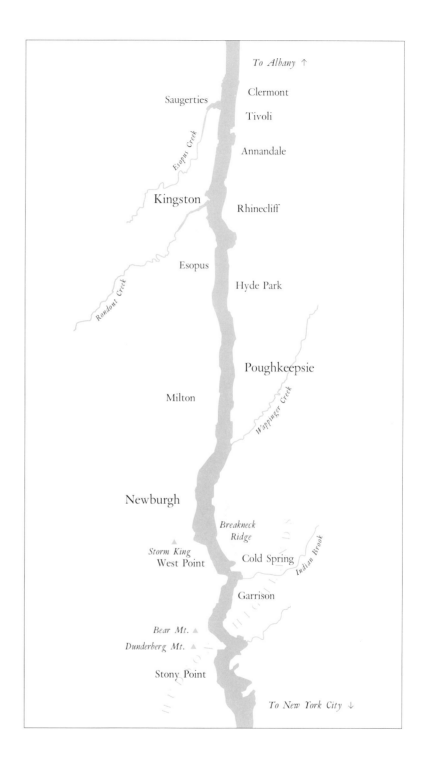

VIEW NORTHWEST FROM HYDE PARK

VIEW SOUTH OF IONA ISLAND FROM BEAR MOUNTAIN

BEAR MOUNTAIN BRIDGE FROM THE TORNE

TUG BOAT AND BARGES BELOW BEAR MOUNTAIN

NIGHT LIGHTS, BEAR MOUNTAIN BRIDGE

SENTINEL, BEAR MOUNTAIN BRIDGE

POPOLOPEN CREEK AND RAILROAD TRESTLE FROM BEAR MOUNTAIN BRIDGE

BEAR MOUNTAIN BRIDGE

SUMMER CLOUDS, IONA BIRD SANCTUARY AND DUNDERBERG MOUNTAIN

SNAKE HOLE CREEK FROM DUNDERBERG MOUNTAIN

SALISBURY MEADOW FROM IONA ISLAND

TREES, GRASSES, BEAR MOUNTAIN

LOVETT POWER PLANT AND FELLED TREES AT STONY POINT

EARLY MORNING FROM ABOVE GARRISON

INDIAN BROOK FALLS, COLD SPRING

CONSTITUTION MARSH AND STORM KING MOUNTAIN

TOWN OF COLD SPRING AND STORM KING

RAILROAD TRACKS AND STORM KING

SHADOW OF STORM KING OVER BREAKNECK RIDGE

TOWN OF CORNWALL FROM STORM KING

STREAM NEAR TIVOLI

WATERFALL AT SAUGERTIES

RONDOUT CREEK AT KINGSTON

OLD DUTCHESS BLEACHERY AT WAPPINGERS FALLS

A HUDSON VIEW, ESOPUS

MAN-MADE POND BESIDE THE HUDSON, ESOPUS

WILL AT VINEYARD, MILTON

OLD RHODE ISLAND GREENING APPLE TREE

1763 FARMHOUSE, MILTON

CONCORD GRAPE VINES, MILTON

CARRIAGE HOUSE AND YELLOW LOCUST TREES, MILTON

ORANGE QUINCE BUSHES

APPLE TREE AND LADDER

CAR TRACKS IN PEAR ORCHARD, EARLY WINTER

VIEW SOUTH FROM MILTON

TRAIN SPEEDING PAST I.B.M., FROM MILTON

BEAN POLES AND LOCUST TREES, MILTON

ARBOR VITAE IN SPRING

RHINECLIFF

A HUDSON VIEW, RHINECLIFF

THE WALLED GARDEN AT BLITHEWOOD, ANANDALE-ON-HUDSON

LATE EVENING, CLERMONT

VIEW NORTH OF BLUE POINT FROM MILTON

VIEW SOUTH OF BLUE POINT FROM THE MID-HUDSON BRIDGE

EVENING FROM BEAR MOUNTAIN

The photographs reproduced in this book
were made between 1985 and 1991.
A commission from the Lila Acheson Wallace Fund
provided initial support.

With thanks also to:
Vida Clift
Oliver, James and Kathleen Kent
Ann and Kingsley Morse
Pari Stave

Among the sources consulted for the text, two were most helpful:
The Hudson by Carl Carmer, and
The Hudson: A Guidebook to the River by Arthur G. Adams.

Library of Congress Catalog Card Number 93–72742
ISBN 0–9618165–1–1

Designed by Catherine Waters
Text set in Van Dijck by Michael and Winifred Bixler
Four impression halftone photography by Robert J. Hennessey
Printed by Susan Medlicott and Emily Oppegard of Allethaire Press
Jacket printed by Meridian Printing
Bound by Acme Bookbinding Company, Inc.

PUBLISHED BY WILLIAM CLIFT EDITIONS

POST OFFICE BOX 6035 · SANTA FE, NEW MEXICO, 87502 · TELEPHONE 505 988–1243